The Best Hashtags for

Luxury Lifestyle

Fitness& Sport,

Fashion & Beauty

on

Instagram, Twitter, Facebook.....

VOLUME 1

CATHERINE-CHANTAL MARANGO

Catherine-chantal Marango

The Best Hashtags for Luxury Lifestyle, Fitness&Sport, Fashion&Beauty on Instagram, Twitter, Facebook ....

Catherine-chantal Marango

The Best Hashtags for

Luxury Lifestyle

Fitness& Sport,

Fashion & Beauty

on

Instagram, Twitter, Facebook.....

VOLUME 1

CATHERINE-CHANTAL MARANGO

Catherine-chantal Marango

The Best Hashtags for Luxury Lifestyle, Fitness&Sport, Fashion&Beauty on Instagram, Twitter, Facebook ….

Catherine-chantal Marango

The Best Hashtags for Luxury Lifestyle, Fitness&Sport, Fashion&Beauty
on Instagram, Twitter, Facebook ....

Catherine-chantal Marango

The Best Hashtags for Luxury Lifestyle, Fitness&Sport, Fashion&Beauty on Instagram, Twitter, Facebook ....

TABLE OF CONTENTS

Catherine-chantal Marango

The Best Hashtags for Luxury Lifestyle, Fitness&Sport, Fashion&Beauty on Instagram, Twitter, Facebook ….

Catherine-chantal Marango

The Best Hashtags for Luxury Lifestyle, Fitness&Sport, Fashion&Beauty on Instagram, Twitter, Facebook ....

Catherine-chantal Marango

Dedication

I dedicate this book to every Person wishing to extend her/his reach on Instagram, Twitter, Facebook and develop successful engagement opportunities

Catherine-chantal Marango

Acknowledgement

I generously thank you Amazon for their active support in publishing my books as well as my family.

Catherine-chantal Marango

More Books by Catherine Chantal Marango

1. You already know French without learning anything: 1000 words that are identical in French and in English

2. Vous connaissez déjà l'anglais sans rien apprendre : les 1000 mots qui sont identiques en français en anglais

3. French at the top : A comparative method between French and English for a speed, easy and successful learning

4. L'anglais sans obstacle : une méthode comparative entre le français et l'anglais pour un apprentissage rapide, facile et sans échec

5. The multilingual dictionary of the most used verbs, adjectives and nouns in French, English, German, Spanish, Italian, Russian and Chinese

6. L'échec n'existe pas : les 3+0 conseils pour toujours réussir en classe et aux examens

7. 30+ killer tips for becoming multilingual without a hitch

8. Les 30+ meilleurs conseils pour devenir multilingue en un clin d'oeil

9. How to overcome all your complexes like a dream

10.   Comment dépasser tous vos complexes

15.The Best Hashtags for the most popular , follow & likes Hashtags, Food and Drinks &Pets and Animals and Flowers on Instagram, Twitter, Facebook, Tik Tok, Volume4

Catherine-chantal Marango

The Best Hashtags for Luxury Lifestyle, Fitness&Sport, Fashion&Beauty on Instagram, Twitter, Facebook ….

Catherine-chantal Marango

The Best Hashtags for Luxury Lifestyle, Fitness&Sport, Fashion&Beauty on Instagram, Twitter, Facebook ....

Introduction

With this encyclopedia of the best hashtags, you can easily extend your reach on Instagram, Twitter, Facebook, Tik Tok and so on , get more engagement on your posts, avoid the hashtag fatigue, consult your hashtags by different categories and insert them into your posts, to find new engagement opportunities and the ultimate branded hashtags. The encyclopedia is in 4 volumes.

Catherine-chantal Marango

The Best Hashtags for Luxury Lifestyle, Fitness&Sport, Fashion&Beauty on Instagram, Twitter, Facebook ....

Catherine-chantal Marango

Chapter 1-Luxury lifestyle Hashtag

a) General luxury lifestyle hashtags

1. #billionaire

2. #billionairelife

3. #billionairelifestyle

4. #fashion

5. #fashionnova

6. #home

7. #instagood

8. #lifestyle

The Best Hashtags for Luxury Lifestyle, Fitness&Sport, Fashion&Beauty
on Instagram, Twitter, Facebook ….

9. #livingluxury

10.   #luxurious

11.   #luxuriouslife

12.   #luxuriouslifestyle

13.   #luxury

14.   #luxury_club

15.   #luxurybag

16.   #luxurybrand

17.   #luxurycar

18.   #luxurycars

19.   #luxurydesign

20.   #luxuryhome

Catherine-chantal Marango

21.   #luxuryhomes

22.   #luxuryhotels

23.   #luxuryhouse

24.   #luxurylife

25.   #luxurylifestyle

26.   #luxurylifestylepix

27.   #luxuryliving

28.   #luxuryrealestate

29.   #luxurytopic

30.   #luxurytravel

31.   #millionaire

32.   #richlife

33.   #wealthylife

34.   #wealthylifestyle

b. Luxury adventures and Top destinations

1. #Alofthotels

2. #bali

3. #borabora

4. #BritishVirginIslands

5. #Dubai

6. #fiji

7. #global Wine Tour

8. #luxuriouscities

9. #luxurucruiselines

10.   #luxuryadventureexcursions

11.   #luxuryadventureexcursions

12.   #Luxuryadventures

13.   #luxurycruiselines

14.   #luxuryoutdoorresort

15.   #luxuryskiresorts

16.   #luxurytravel

17.   #monaco

18.   #SkyHighHotAirBalloonFestival

19.   #Skyhighluxury

Catherine-chantal Marango

20.   #starstrips

21.   #tuscany

22.   #ultraluxury

23.   #Ultraluxury cruise

24.   #ultraluxurycruiseline

25.   #VolcanoExpedition

26.   #Luxuryskiresorts

27.   VistaJet World

c. Luxury transport hashtags

- **Luxury Cars Hashtag**

1. #automotive

The Best Hashtags for Luxury Lifestyle, Fitness&Sport, Fashion&Beauty on Instagram, Twitter, Facebook ….

2. #amazingcars

3. #Battistaanniversariocars

4. #cargram

5. #carlifestyle

6. #carlovers

7. #carphotography

8. #carsofinstagram

9. #carstagram

10.   #carwithoutlimits

11.   #fastcars

12.   #hypercar

13.   #hypercars

Catherine-chantal Marango

The Best Hashtags for Luxury Lifestyle, Fitness&Sport, Fashion&Beauty on Instagram, Twitter, Facebook ....

14.   #instacar

15.   #instacars

16.   #Karma Automotive

17.   #lexus

18.   #Lincoln SUVs

19.   #luxurycars

20.   #Maserati'

21.   #Porsche911TurboS

22.   #Shouqi Limousine

23.   #sportcar

24.   #sportscar

25.   #supercars

Catherine-chantal Marango

The Best Hashtags for Luxury Lifestyle, Fitness&Sport, Fashion&Beauty on Instagram, Twitter, Facebook ....

- **Boat hashtags**

1. #arcadiayachts

2. # riva

3. # theblackswan

4. #420-footUniqueCircle

5. #60 Cantius

6. #BaylinerElement

7. #beneteauoceanis

8. #Bennington22GL

9. #bertram

10.   #boat

Catherine-chantal Marango

The Best Hashtags for Luxury Lifestyle, Fitness&Sport, Fashion&Beauty on Instagram, Twitter, Facebook ….

11.   #boating

12.   #boating

13.   #boatinglife

14.   #boatlife

15.   #boats

16.   #boatshow

17.   #Bonettioasis135

18.   #bostonwhaler

19.   #cabincruiser

20.   #canoe

21.   #catamaran

22.   #chapparal

Catherine-chantal Marango

23.   #cruise

24.   #cruiselife

25.   #crystalblue

26.   #dufouryachts

27.   #DynamiqGTT115

28.   #flyingyacht

29.   #FourWinnsH180

30.   #jeanneau

31.   #Johnson110

32.   #kayak

33.   #krogenopen50

34.   #leopard48

35. #lund

36. #luxuryyacht

37. #megayacht

38. #miamiyachtshow

39. #montecarlo6

40. #motorboat

41. #motoryacht

42. #needforspeed

43. #oceanis55

44. #Passengercarriers

45. #powercruiser

46. #regulator41

47. #ridingthewind

48. #rivarace

49. #runabouts

50. #sailing

51. #sailingship

52. #sailpower

53. #sea

54. #Sea-DooWakePro230

55. #searay

56. #SeaRay470

57. #SeaRayL650Fly

58. #shiplife#sailinglife

59.   #Solaris50

60.   #Steamship

61.   #Submarine

62.   #superyacht

63.   #Tahoe450

64.   #tracker

65.   #vikingyachts

66.   #WaverunnerVX

67.   #Workingships17

68.   #Worldofwatercraft

69.   #yacht

70.   #yachtcharter

71.   #yachtclub

72.   #yachtdesign

73.   #yachting

74.   #yachtlife

75.   #yachts

76.   #yachtworld

77.   #yamaha

78.   Rivayachts

- ### Luxury Aviation Hashtags

1. airplane

2. #avgeek

3. #aviation

4. #aviationdaily

5. #aviationlovers

6. #aviationphotography

7. #avphotography

8. #businessaviation

9. dubaiairshow

10.   #dukejets

11.   #Electricairplane

12.   #flyprivate

13.   #instagramaviation

14.   #instajet

The Best Hashtags for Luxury Lifestyle, Fitness&Sport, Fashion&Beauty on Instagram, Twitter, Facebook ….

15.   #instaflying

16.   #instaplane

17.   #jetlife

18.   #GuflstreamG500

19.   #GuflstreamG600

20.   #MEBAAShow

21.   #megaplane

22.   #planespotting

23.   #privatejet

24.   #privatejetlife

25.   #privatejettravel

26.   #volocopterairtaxi

Catherine-chantal Marango

The Best Hashtags for Luxury Lifestyle, Fitness&Sport, Fashion&Beauty on Instagram, Twitter, Facebook ….

d. Luxury Events

1. #Wine events

2. #AGTA

3. #Annapolisboatshow

4. #Arlequi Wine Merchant

5. #AsleyLynnWinery

6. #birkiefestival

7. #Boat Events

8. #bride

9. #brideandgroom

10. #bridetobe

11. #Brideworldexpo

12. #Copadelrey

13. #corporateevents

14. #entertainment

15. #EPHJ-EPMT-SMT Show

16. #eventdecor

17. #eventdesign

18. #eventplanning

19. #eventprofs

20. #events

21.   #eventstyling

22.   #FashionKode

23.   #fineartasia

24.   #fineartfair

25.   #flowers

26.   #Garagiste festival

27.   #greenfestival

28.   #Gresystonemansion

29.   #Growtech

30.   #IBEX

31.   #IJL

32.   #internationalbeautyexpo

33.   #internationaLCTtour

34.   #lajolla

35.   #Lapadaart

36.   #Laromaine

37.   #LaWineFest

38.   #LCT-NLA show

39.   #luxepackmonaco

40.   #luxurydecor

41.   #luxurydress

42.   #luxuryevents

43.   #luxurygoods

44.   #luxurylawsummit

Catherine-chantal Marango

45.   #luxuryresort

46.   #luxurywedding

47.   #luxuryweddings

48.   #maisonet objetsparis

49.   #Mayfair

50.   #Monaco Yacht Show

51.   #moscowgolfshow

52.   #Moscowinternationalpropertyshow

53.   #neuroplanet

54.   #nycevents

55.   #party

56.   #Pebble beach food and wine event

57.   #premièrevisionparis

58.   #privatevent

59.   #Rowingregatta

60.   #SanDiego BayWine

61.   #SanDiego boatShow

62.   #SAP/asug Conference

63.   #SavorBlowingRock

64.   #SingaporeRendezVous

65.   #specialevents

66.   #thearmoryshow

67.   #wedding

68.   #weddinginspiration

69.   #weddingplanner

70.   #women'sexpo

71.   #worldluxuryexpo

e. Luxury trendy skincare and brands

1. #CIREM

2. # La Mer The Rejuvenating Hand Serum

3. # NuFace Mini Facial Toning Device

4. # Shiseido Future Solution LX Replenishing Treatment Oil

5. # SK-II Facial Treatment Essence

6. # The Dewy Skin Cream

7. # Victoria Beckham by Augustinus Bader Cell Rejuvenating Priming Moisturizer

8. #allnatural

9. #AmorePacific Youth Revolution Radiance Concentrator

10.   #Elemis

11.   #Formula Z Cosmetics launches NEW Luxe Diamond Lip Glosses

12.   #formulazcosmetics

13.   #formulazcosmeticslipgloss

14.   #herbivore

15.   #herbivoreprismlotion

16.   #La Prairie Platinum Rare Cellular Life

Lotion

17.   #lamer

18.   #laprairie

19.   #lawless

20.   #Lina Hanson Organic Global Treasures

Eye/Neck

21.   #luxediamondlipgloss

22.   #LuxuryAll-NaturalCosmetics

23.   #LuxuryBeautyProducts

24.   #Luxurycosmetics

25.   #SK-II mask

26.   #SK-II Overnight Miracle Mask

27.   #Tatcha

f.Luxury cuisine hashtags

1. #10cane

2. #Agropur

3. #Agropurbestcheddar

4. #alainducasse

5. #Angelsenvystraightbourbonwhiskey

6. #Angulas

7. #Appleton Estate

8. #Ass Cheese/pule

9. #BestCheddar

10.   #Black Densuke Watermelons

11.   #bluebyalainducasse

12.   #bourbon

13.   #boxedwater

14.   #Château Élan Winery & Resort

15.   #chefalainducasse

16.   #Culatella di Zibello

17.   #DelilleCellars

18.   #Dewardsillegalsmooth

19.   #Edible gold leaves

20.   #food art

21.   #food insights

22.   #food trends

Catherine-chantal Marango

23.   #Fornodeminas

24.   #Fugu

25.   #geramin-robin

26.   #heavendoorspirits

27.   #Italian White Alba Truffle

28.   #Kobebeef

29.   #LOUIS XIII COGNAC

30.   #luxury event

31.   #luxury food

32.   #luxurydisposable

33.   #Macallan   55-year-old   Single   Malt

    Whisky

34.   #magnumruby

35.   #Matsutake Mushrooms

36.   #Minerfamilywinery

37.   #Pullmanwinebar

38.   #RegiisOva

39.   #Saffron

40.   #signaturekitchen

41.   #spirits

42.   #Stag's Leap Wine Cellars

43.   #thegentlivet

44.   #Wagyu Beef

45.   #whiskey

46.   #whiskeycollection

47. #whiskeycollectionheavendoorspirits

48. #Whitetruffles

49. #wine

50. #winecellar

51. #winemakingexcellence

52. #wineryresort

53. #Yubari King Melons

54. #zchocolat

g. Best gourmet luxuries and brands hashtags

1. #Harrods

2. #AngelinaParis

3. #Fortnumandmason

4. #HarveyNicols

5. #LaduréeParis

6. #Ritz

7. #rougié

8. #selfridgandco

9. #thewholseley

10. #Valrhona

h.Luxury home decor and furniture hashtags

1. #luxuryhome

2. #Bookends

3. #LuxuryBaskets

4. #LuxuryBathLinen

5. #luxuryBathroomDecor

6. #LuxuryBedLinen

7. #LuxuryBedspreads

8. #LuxuryBlankets

9. #LuxuryBlankets

10.   #LuxuryBooks

11.   #LuxuryCandles

12.   #LuxuryCardGames

13.   #LuxuryCushions

14.   #LuxuryDiffusers

15.   #LuxuryDuvetCovers

16.   #luxuryFaux Flowers

17.   #luxuryhomedecoraccessories

18.   #LuxuryHOMEFRAGRANCE

Catherine-chantal Marango

19. #LuxuryHurricaneLamps

20. #LuxuryMirrors

21. #LuxuryOrnaments

22. #LuxuryPhoto Frames

23. #LuxurySculptures

24. #LuxurySheets

25. #LuxurySleepware

26. #LuxuryThrows

27. #LuxuryVases

28. #LuxuryWallArt

29. #LUXURYLIVINGROOM

30. #LuxurySofas

Catherine-chantal Marango

31.   #LuxuryArmchairs

32.   #LuxurySideTables

33.   #LuxuryCoffeeTables

34.   #LuxuryConsole Tables

35.   #LuxuryGameTables

36.   #LuxuryBEDROOM

37.   #LuxuryBeds

38.   #LuxuryBedsideTables

39.   #LuxuryDressingTables

40.   #LuxuryWardrobes

41.   #LuxuryDINING ROOM

42.   #LuxuryDiningTables

43.   #LuxuryDining Chairs

44.   #LuxurySideboards

45.   #LuxuryCabinets

46.   #LuxuryDrinksCabinets

47.   #LuxuryBar

48.   # LuxuryCounterStools

49.   #LuxuryTrolleys

50.   #LuxuryDesks

51.   #LuxuryOffice Chairs

52.   #LuxuryBookcases

53.   #LUXURYOUTDOOR COLLECTION

54.   #LuxuryOutdoorLivingFurniture

55.   #LuxuryOutdoorDiningFurniture

i.Luxury watches hashtags

1. #Luxurywatches

2. #AudemarsPiguetRoyalOakQuartz

3. #Bell & Ross BR S Rose Gold watch

4. #BellandRossVintageV2-93

5. #BlancpainFiftyFathoms

6. #BlancpainFiftyFathomsMeteorAutomatic

7. #BulgariOcto41mm

8. #Cartier Tank Solo

9. #CartierDrivedeCartier

10.   #ChanelMonsieurWatch

11. #Chopard Imperiale watch

12. #ChopardMilleMigliaRacing

13. #Designa Individual

14. #GirardPerregauxLaureato

15. #HublotBigBang

16. #IWC Portofino Automatic Day & Night

37

17. #IWCPortugueseAutomaticChronograp

h

18. #Jaeger-LeCoultreMasterUltraThinMoon

19. #Limelight Gala watch by Piaget

20. #Little Lange 1 Moon Phase watch by

A.Lange & Söhne

Catherine-chantal Marango

21.   #MontblancTimewalkerUrban

22.   #OmegaSpeedmasterRacingAutomatic

23.   #ParmigianiFleurierToricHemispheresRetrograde

24.   #Patek Nautilus 7010/1R-011

25.   #PatekPhilippeGrandComplications

26.   #PiagetAltiplano

27.   #Quantieme Retrograde by Blancpain

28.   #RadoDiamaster

29.   #Rolex Pearlmaster 34

30.   #RolexCosmographDaytona

31.   #RolexExplorer II

32.   #SmallModelwatchbyVacheronConstant

   in

33.   #VacheronConstantinOverseas

34.   #ZenithElPrimero

35.   #ZenithElPrimeroChronomaster1969

Chapter 2 -Transport Hashtags (Cars, Boats, Planes)

a. The best general hashtags for Cars

1. #13b

2. #180sx

3. #1jz

4. #1le

5. #240sx

6. #2jz

7. #350z

8. #370z

9. #3series

10.   #420-footUniqueCircle

11.   #458

12.   #4wd

13.   #60 Cantius

14.   #abarth

15.   #abarth500

16.   #Actros

17.   #ae86

18.   #ae86

19.   #amazingcars

20.   #amazing_cars

21.   #amazingcars247

22.   #amg

23.   #ar

24.   #astonmartin

25.   #AstonMartin Vanquish

26.   #astra

27.   #audi

28.   #audiofficial

29.   #audigramm

30.   #audilove

31.   #audination

32.   #audir8

33.   #audisport

34.   #audiTT

35.   #audizine

36.   #austinmini

37.   #auto

38.   #autogespot

39.   #autokings

40.   #automobile

41.   #automotive

42.   #autos

43.   #autotrend

44.   #aventador

45.   #awd

46.   #bagged

47.   #bajucowok

48.   #bajukonveksi

49.   #bajukorea

50.   #bajusale

51.   #barro

52.   #Bayliner Element

53.   #bbs

54.   #beetle

55.   #BelgianGP

56.   #beneteauoceanis

57.   #Bennington 22GL

58.   #bentley

59.   #benz

60.   #bertram

61.   #bigsize

62.   #billionaire

63.   #bimmer

64.   #black_list

65.   #bluebird

66.   #bmc

67.   #bmw

68.   #bmwgram

69.   #bmwlife

70.   #bmwlove

71.   #bmwm

72.   #bmwm3

73.   #bmwmini

74.   #bmwnation

75.   #bmwrepost

76.   #Bonettioasis135

77.   #bostonwhaler

78.   #Bowriders

79.   #bpa_rides

80.   #bringthenoise

81.   #brz

82.   #bug

83.   #bugatti

84.   #bugattiveyron

85.   #c10

86.   #c7

87.   #cabincruiser

88.   #Cad i l lacEldorado

89.   #cadillac

90.   #camaro

91.   #camaross

92.   #canoe

93.   #caprice

94.   #car

95.   #cargram

96.   #cargramm

97.   #carinstagram

98.   #carlifestyle

99.   #cars

100.   #carsofinstagram

101.   #carspotting

102.   #carstagram

103.   #carswithoutlimits

104.   #chapparal

105.   #cherokee

106.   #chevrolet

107.   #chevroletcorvette

108.   #chevy

109.   #chevycamaro

110.   #chevylife

111.   #chevyrunsdeep

112.   #chevytruck

113.   #choraboy

114.   #cj

115.   #classicar

116.   #classicmini

117.   #clublexus

118.   #clubman

119.   #cobra

120.   #Convertibles

121.   #cooper

122.   #corsa

123.   #corvette

124.   #Crazy cars

125.   #crystalblue

126.   #cummins

127.   #daf

128.   #dailylexus

129.   #datsun

130.   #diesel

131.   #dodge

132.   #dollhouse

133.   #Dragsterburnout

134.   #dreamcar

135.   #dreamcars

136.   #drift

137.   #driftcar

138.   #drifter

139.   #drifting

140.   #driftlife

141.   #drive

142.   #driver

143.   #dub

144.   #ducati

145.   #dufouryachts

146.   #dunebuggy

147.   #duramax

148.   #Dynamiq GTT 115

149.   #e30

150.   #e36

151.   #e46

152.   #Easyriders

153.   #electriccar

154.   #engine

155.   #eunos

156.   #ev

157.   #evo

158.   #evo9

159.   #evox

160.   #exotic

161.   #exoticcar

162.   #exoticcars

163.   #f1

164.   #F12016

165.   #f150

166.   #f250

167.   #fairlady

168.   #fairladyz

169.   #Familycars

170.   #fast

171.   #Fastandfurious

172.   #fastcar

173.   #fastcars

174. #Fasterandfaster

175. #fd3s

176. #feelinggood

177. #ferrari

178. #Ferrari F2008

179. #Ferrarienzo

180. #fh16

181. #fiat500

182. #fixa

183. #fj

184. #ford

185. #fordmustang

186. #fordracing

187.   #fordsofinstagram

188.   #forester

189.   #formel1

190.   #formula1

191.   #formuladrift

192.   #FormulaOne

193.   #FormulaUno

194.   #Formule1

195.   #ForzaFerrari

196.   #ForzaSeb

197.   #Four Winns H180

198.   #freeway

199.   #frs

200.   #fsport

201.   #fsportsociety

202.   #ft86

203.   #fusca

204.   #g35

205.   #g37

206.   #gamismurah

207.   #gm

208.   #gmc

209.   #godzilla

210.   #golf

211.   #golfr

212.   #grandprix

213.   #gs300

214.   #gt

215.   #gt500

216.   #gt86

217.   #gti

218.   #gtr

219.   #gtspirit

220.   #highway

221.   #hilux

222.   #honda

223.   #hoonigan

224.   #horsepower

225.   #hypercar

226.   #hypercars

227.   #hyundai

228.   #impreza

229.   #infiniti

230.   #instaauto

231.   #instacar

232.   #instacars

233.   #is250

234.   #is300

235.   #is350

236.   #isf

237.   #itsajeepthing

238.   #itswhitenoise

239.   #iveco

240.   #jaguar

241.   #jcw

242.   #jdm

243.   #jdmgram

244.   #jeanneau

245.   #jeep

246.   #jeepbeef

247.   #jeepfamily

248.   #jeepgirl

249.   #jeepher

250.   #jeepin

251.   #jeepjk

252.   #jeeplife

253.   #jeeplove

254.   #jeepnation

255.   #jeeps

256.   #jeepthing

257.   #jeepwrangler

258.   #jetta

259.   #jk

260.   #jku

261.   #kayak

262.   #kenworth

263.   #kia

264.   #KimiRaikkonen

265.   #kingoftheroad

266.   #kouki

267.   #krogenopen50

268.   #laferrari

269.   #lambo

270.   #lamborghini

271.   #landcruiser

272.   #leopard48

273.   #lewishamilton

274.   #lexus

275.   #lexusboys

276.   #lexusis

277.   #lexuslife

278.   #lexuslove

279.   #lexusnation

280.   #lifted

281.   #Lincoln-Zephyr

282.   #low

283.   #ls3

284.   #ls9

285.   #lsx

286.   #Lund

287.   #lux

288.   #luxe

289.   #luxlife

290.   #luxurious

291.   #Luxury rides

292.   #luxury4play

293.   #luxurycar

294.   #luxurycars

295.   #luxurylife

296.   #luxurylifestyle

297.   #luxuryliving

298.   #luxurystyle

299.   #luxurytravel

300.   #lx570

301.   #m3

302.   #m4

303.   #m5

304.   #Machineswithstyle

305.   #madwhips

306.   #maserati

307.   #mastercraft

308.   #mazda

309.   #mazda3

310.   #mazda6

311.   #mazdafitment

312.   #mazdaflow

313.   #mazdamiata

314.   #mazdamovement

315.   #mazdanation

316.   #mazdaspeed

317.   #mazdaspeed3

318.   #mb

319.   #Mcclaren

320.   #McclarenF1

321.   #mclaren

322.   #merc

323.   #mercedes

324.   #mercedesamg

325.   #mercedesamgf1

326.   #mercedesbenz

327.   #miata

328.   #miatagang

329.   #millionaire

330.   #millionairelifestyle

331.   #Minimotors

332.   #miniature

333.   #miniatures

334.   #miniclub

335.   #minicooper

336.   #minicoopers

337.   #minifamily

338.   #minijcw

339.   #minilove

340.   #minimag

341.   #minis

342.   #minisofinstagram

343.   #mitsubishi

344.   #mk2

345.   #mk3

346.   #mk4

347.   #mk5

348.   #mk6

349.   #mk7

350.   #modelx

351.   #Modernwarships

352.   #montecarlo6

353.   #monza

354.   #mopar

355.   #Mopettamicrocar

356.   #motogp

357.   #motor

358.   #motorhead_

359.   #motorboat

360.   #motorracing

361.   #motors

362.   #motorsport

363.   #motorsports

364.   #mperformance

365.   #mpower

366.   #ms3

367.   #muffler

368.   #murmer

369.   #mustang

370.   #mustangfanclub

371.   #mustanggt

372.   #mustangsofinstagram

373.   #mx5

374.   #Needforspeed

375.   #nicorosberg

376.   #nismo

377.   #nissan

378.   #nissangtr

379.   #oceanis55

380.   #offroad

381.   #ohsoretro

382.   #ohsoretroevents

383.   #olive

384.   #onlinetrust

385.   #opc

386.   #opel

387.   #pagani

388.   #Passengercarriers

389.   #peterbilt

390.   #Pioneering cars

391.   #pontiac

392.   #porsche

393.   #porsche911

394.   #powercruiser

395.   #powerstroke

396.   #PrancingHorse

397.   #quattro

398.   #r33

399.   #r34

400.   #r35

401.   #r730

402.   #r8

403.   #race

404.   #racecars

405.   #racecar

406.   #racing

407.   #rally

408.   #rallycar

409.   #rallycross

410.   #rallye

411.   #rangerover

412.   #Record breakers

413.   #redbullracing

414.   #RedSeason

415.   #regulator41

416.   #renault

417.   #rich

418.   #ride

419.   #Ridingthewind

420.   #rim

421.   #rims

422.   #road

423.   #roadster

424.   #rollsroyce

425.   #rotary

426.	#rs4

427.	#rs5

428.	#rs6

429.	#rs7

430.	#rubicon

431.	#rumblebros

432.	#Runabouts

433.	#rx7

434.	#rx8

435.	#s13

436.	#s13

437.	#s14

438.   #s15

439.   #s550

440.   #Sailingship

441.   #Sailpower

442.   #sc300

443.   #scania

444.   #schassis

445.   #scion

446.   #scuderia

447.   #scuderiaferrari

448.   #Sea-DooWakePro230

449.   #searay

450.   #SeaRay470.

451.   #SeaRayL65 Fly

452.   #Seb5

453.   #SebastianVettel

454.   #SebVettel

455.   #shelby

456.   #silverado

457.   #silvia

458.   #skyline

459.   #slammed

460.   #sline

461.   #soarer

462.   #Solaris50

463.   #spafrancorchamps

464.   #speed

465.   #spoiler

466.   #sportcar

467.   #sportscars

468.   #sportscar

469.   #sportscar

470.   #sr20

471.   #srt

472.   #ss

473.   #stance

474.   #stanced

475.   #stancenation

476.   #stang

477.   #Steamship

478.   #sti

479.   #Streetcars

480.   #subaru

481.   #subaru

482.   #subarulove

483.   #subarunation

484.   #subaruwrx

485.   #subie

486.   #subie001

487.   #subiedaily

488.   #subieflow

489.   #subiegang

490.   #subielove

491.   #subienation

492.   #Submarine

493.   #supercar

494.   #Supercars

495.   #supercarsdaily700

496.   #supercarsoflondon

497.   #supercross

498.   #supra

499.   #suprememodellista

500.   #SV5

501.   #svt

502.   #tacoma

503.   #Tahoe 450

504.   #TeamVettel

505.   #tesla

506.   #teslamodels

507.   #teslamotors

508.   #tire

509.   #tires

510.   #tj

511.   #topmiata

512.   #toyota

513.   #tracker

514.   #transport

515.   #trd

516.   #Truck

517.   #tundra

518.   #turbo

519.   #ukm

520.   #ukminis

521.   #v8

522.   #vauxhall

523.   #vdub

524.   #vehicle

525.   #vehicles

526.   #Vettel

527.   #vikingyachts

528.   #vintagecars

529.   #vipstylecars

530.   #vocho

531.   #volks

532.   #volkswagen

533.   #volkswagenbeetle

534.   #volvo

535.   #volvocars

536.   #volvofamily

537.   #volvoforlife

538.   #volvolove

539.   #volvomoment

540.   #volvotrucks

541.   #vw

542.   #vwbeetle

543.   #vwbug

544.   #vwbus

545.   #vwgolf

546.   #vwlife

547.   #vwlove

548.   #vwvortex

549.   #Waverunner VX

550.   #wheel

551.   #wheels

552.   #whip

553.   #wrangler

554.   #wrc

555.   #wrx

556.   #wrxsti

557.   #xj

558.   #yamaha

559.   #yj

560.   #yota

561.   #z28

562.   #z33

563.   #zenki

564.   #zl1

565.   #zoomzoom

566.   #zr1

b. **Boat Hashtags**

1. # theblackswan

2. #420-footUniqueCircle

3. #60 Cantius

4. #Aircraftcarriers

5. #BaylinerElement

6. #beneteauoceanis

7. #Bennington22GL

8. #bertram

9. #Bonettioasis135

The Best Hashtags for Luxury Lifestyle, Fitness&Sport, Fashion&Beauty on Instagram, Twitter, Facebook ....

10.   #bostonwhaler

11.   #Bowriders

12.   #cabincruiser

13.   #canoe

14.   #catamaran

15.   #chapparal

16.   #crystalblue

17.   #dufouryachts

18.   #Dynamiq TT 115

19.   #Four WinnsH180

20.   #jeanneau

21.   #kayak

Catherine-chantal Marango

22.   #krogenopen50

23.   #leopard48

24.   #Lund

25.   #mastercraft

26.   #Modern warships

27.   #montecarlo6

28.   #motorboat

29.   #Needforspeed

30.   #oceanis55

31.   #Passengercarriers

32.   #powercruiser

33.   #regulator41

34.   #Ridingthewind

35.   #Runabouts

36.   #Sailingship

37.   #Sailpower

38.   #Sea RayL650Fly

39.   #Sea-DooWakePro 230

40.   #searay

41.   #SeaRay470

42.   #Solaris 50

43.   #Steamship

44.   #Submarine

45.   #superyacht

46.   #Tahoe 450

47.   #tracker

48.   #vikingyachts

49.   #Waverunner VX

50.   #wildernessraft

51.   #Workingships 17

52.   #Worldofwatercraft

53.   #yacht

54.   #yamaha

c.Plane Hashtags

1. #737

2. #airbus

3. Airbus Helicopters

4. #Airbus A220

5. #airbusA220

6. #airbusA320neo

7. #airbusA350

8. #airbus380

9. #aircraft

10.   #aircraftcarriers

11.   #airline

12.   #airplane

13.   #airport

14.   #Airsupport

15.   #Astar

16.   #avgeek

17.   #aviation

18.   #aviationdaily

19.   #aviationgeek

20.   #aviationlovers

21.   #aviationphotography

22.   #avphotography

23.   #boeing

24.   #Boeing767

25.   #Boeing787

26.   #Dreamliner

27.   #boeing737

28.   #boeinglovers

29.   #cougar

30.   #Dauphin

31.   #ECO-Star (EC-130)

32.   #Eurocopter3 X

33.   #Eyesinthesky

34.   #Fighterplanes

35.   #flight

36.   #fly

37.   #flying

38.   #Helicopter

39.   #instaaviation

40.   #instagramaviation

41.   #instaplane

42.   #jet

43.   #Jetfighters

44.   #lax

45.   #Lightaircraft 218

46.   #luxury

47.   #megaplane

48.   #panther

49.   #pilot

50.   #pilotlife

51.   #plane

52.   #planes

53.   #planespotter

54.   #planespotting

55.   #privatejet

56.   #puma

57.   #Seaplanes

58.   #sky

59.   #spotting

60.   #Strikeforce

61.   #superpuma

62.   #Superspeed

63.   #travel

64.   #Twinstar

65.   #Whirlybirds

66.   #Workingchoppers

Chapter 3-Fitness and sport Hashtags

a. Sports Hashtags

1. #action

2. #active

3. #ball

4. #balls

5. #baseball

6. #basketball

7. #Basketball

8. #Boxing

9. #Cricket

10.	#crowd

11.	#Cycling

12.	#fans

13.	#field

14.	#fit

15.	#football

16.	#fun

17.	#game

18.	#games

19.   #goal

20.   #grass

21.   #green

22.   #Hockey

23.   #kick

24.   #pass

25.   #play

26.   #player

27.   #playing

28.   #Rugby

29.   #Skateboarding

30.   #Skiing

31.   Snowboarding

32.   #Soccer

33.   #sport

34.   #sports

35.   #Surfing

36.   #Swimming

37.   #Tennis

38.   #throw

39.   #Ultimate Frisbee

40.   #Volleyball

41.   #win

42.   #winning

43.   #Wrestling

b. General hashtags for fitness

1. #abs

2. #active

3. #aerobictraining

4. #aesthetics

5. #Barbells

6. #beastmode

7. #bestoftheday

8. #body

9. #bodybuilder

a. #bodyweighttraining

10. #BodyweightTraining

11. #bulkingtips

12. #carbohydrateintake

13. #cardio

14. #Chin-up

15. #cleaneating

16. #crossfit

17. #dedication

18. #diet

19. #Dumbellweighttraining

20. #eatclean

21. #exercise

22. #exercisetime

23. #fitfam

24. #fitfreak

25. #fitgirl

26. #fitgoals

27. #fitlife

28. #fitnessaddict

29. #fitnessaddiction

30. #fitnessfreak

31. #fitnessmodel

32. #fitnessmotivation

33. #fitspiration

Catherine-chantal Marango

34.   #fitspirational

35.   #fitspo

36.   #gains

37.   #getbigandbulky

38.   #getfit

39.   #getmoving

40.   #getstronger

41.   #girlswholift

42.   #girlswholiftheavy

43.   #gym

44.   #gymlife

45.   #health

46.   #healthylife

47.   #heretocreate

48.   #HIIT

49.   #instadaily

50.   #instafit

51.   #instafitfam

52.   #instafitness

53.   #instafitsociety

54.   #instahealth

55.   #justrun

56.   #lifestyle

57.   #liftingprogram

a. #Machineweighttraining

58.	#muscle

59.	#muscles

60.	#muscularpotential

61.	#nopainnogain

62.	#nopainnogains

63.	#nutrition

64.	#olympicweightlifting

65.	#physicalgoals

66.	#physique

67.	#proteinintake

68.	#Resistance bands

69.	#Row

70.   #runspiration

71.   #shredded

72.   #starttraining

73.   #stopexercising

74.   #strength

75.   #strong

76.   #thesweatlife

77.   #trainingdays

78.   #twelveskip

79.   #weightloss

80.   #whyirun

81.   #yoga

82.   #youcandoittoo

c.Fitness food hashtags

1. #cleaneating

2. #cleaneats

3. #cleanfood

4. #dedication

5. #determination

6. #diet

7. #dietasemsofrer

8. #dietfood

9. #eatforabs

10. #eathealthy

11. #eatingclean

12. #essentialfood

13. #fearfatclub

14. #fitfood

15. #fitfoodie

16. #fitforlife

17. #fitnessaddict

18. #fitnessfood

19. #flexibledieting

20. #foodisfuel

21. #getfit

Catherine-chantal Marango

22.   #glutenfree

23.   #healthybreakfast

24.   #healthychoice

25.   #healthychoices

26.   #healthydiet

27.   #healthyeating

28.   #healthyeating

29.   #healthyfood

30.   #healthyfoodshare

31.   #healthylife

32.   #healthylifestyle

33.   #healthymary

34.   #healthymeal

35.   #healthyrecipes

36.   #healthysnack

37.   #lowcarb

38.   #muscle

39.   #nutrition

40.   #protein

41.   #realfood

42.   #saudável

43.   #shredded

44.   #veganfood

45.   #weightloss

Catherine-chantal Marango

46.   #Fiber

47.   #GoodFats

48.   #Minerals

49.   #Omega-3 (EPA & DHA)

50.   # Protein

51.   #{Starches

52.   #berries

53.   #spice

54.   #Anchovies

55.   #Apple

56.   #Arugula

57.   #Asparagus

58.   #AvocadoOil

59.   #Avocado

60.   #Banana

61.   #Basil

62.   #Beef

63.   #Beet

64.   #BellPepper

65.   #Beverages

66.   #Bison

67.   #BlackCoffee

68.   *#BokChoy*

69.   #Broccoli

70.   #BrusselsSprout

71.   #Butter

72.   #Cabbage

73.   #Cantaloupe

74.   #Cardamom

75.   #Carrot

76.   #Cauliflower

77.   #CayennePepper

78.   #Chard

79.   #Cherry

80.   #Chicken

81.   #ChiliPowder

82.   #Cilantro

83.   #Parsley

84.   #Cinnamon

85.   #Clams

86.   #Cloves

87.   #CoconutWater

88.   #Coconut

89.   #CollardGreens

90.   #Coriander

91.   #Crab

92.   #Cucumber

93.   #Cumin

94.   #Curry

95.   #Eggs

96.   #ExtraVirginOliveOil

97.   #Fennel

98.   #Flax Oil

99.   #Fruits

100.   #GarlicPowder

101.   #Garlic

102.   #Ghee

103.   #Ginger

104.   #Grapes

105.   #Guava

106.   #Kale

107.   #Kiwi

108.   #Lamb

109.   #Leek

110.   #Lemon

111.   #Lime

112.   #Lemon

113.   #LimeJuice

114.   #Lettuce

115.   #Liver

116.   #Lobster

117.   #Mackerel

118.   #Mango

119.   #Mushroom

120.   #Mustard Powder

121.   #Nutmeg

122.   #OnionPowder

123.   #Onion

124.   #Orange

125.   #Oregano

126.   #Oysters

127.   #PalmOil

128.   #Paprika

129.   #Peach

130.   #Pear

131.   #Pepper

132.   #Pineapple

133.   #Plum

134.   #Pomegranate

135.   #Pork

136.   #Potato

137.   #Radish

138.   #RedPepperFlakes

139.   #Rosemary

140.   #Sage

141.   #Salmon

142.   #Salt

143.   #Sardines

144.   #Shrimp

145.   #Spinach

146.   #Squash

147.   #SweetPotato

148.   #Tallow

149.   #Tea

150.   #Thyme

151.   #Tomato

152.   #Trout

153.   #Tuna

154.   #Turkey

155.   #Turmeric

156.   #Venison

157.   #Vinegar

158.   #Virgin Coconut Oil

159.   #vitamins

160.   Walnut Oil

161.   #Water

162.   #Watermelon

163.   #Yam

The Best Hashtags for Luxury Lifestyle, Fitness&Sport, Fashion&Beauty on Instagram, Twitter, Facebook ....

Catherine-chantal Marango

Chapter 4- Fashion hashtags

a.Fashion general hashtags

1. #accessories

2. #beautydoesnthavetobepain

3. #casual

4. #casualchic

5. #chic

6. #classy

7. #classyclothes

8. #clothes

9. #currentwearing

10. #designer

11. #dressofthe day

12. #effortlesschic

13. #everydaymadewell

14. #fancyclothes

15. #fashion

16. #Fashion

17. #Fashion Marketing

18. #fashionable

19. #Fashionable

20. #fashionaddict

21. #fashionblog

22.   #fashionblogger

23.   #FashionCollections

24.   #fashiondesigners

25.   #fashiondiaries

26.   #FashionDolls

27.   #FashionEditors

28.   #fashionevents

29.   #fashiongoals

30.   #fashiongram

31.   #FashionIcons

32.   #FashionIllustrators

33.   #FashionIndustry

34.   #fashionista

35.   #fashionkilla

36.   #FashionMagazines

37.   #FashionModels

38.   #FashionMuseums

39.   #FashionOnline

40.   #FashionPhotography

41.   #FashionPlates

42.   #fashionpost

43.   #fashionprops

44.   #FashionShows

45.   #fashionstyle

46.   #fashionstyle

47.   #fashionstyle

48.   #FashioTnelevision

49.   #fashionweek

50.   #Frenchchic

51.   #girly

52.   #hairstyle

53.   #hautecouture

54.   #highendfashion

55.   #Hiphopfashion

56.   #igooutfit

57.   #instafashion

58.   #instagood

59.   #instaoutfit

60.   #instastyle

61.   #Italianchic

62.   #Italianfashion

63.   #jewelry

64.   #justaddsole

65.   #like

66.   #lookbook

67.   #lookgoodfeelgood

68.   #lookoftheday

69.   #love

70.   #lovethislook

71.   #luxury

72.   #madewell

73.   #menstyle

74.   #menswear

75.   #menwithstyle

76.   #moda

77.   #model

78.   #mrporterlive

79.   #onlineshopping

80.   #ootd

81.   #ootdfash

82.   #ootdinspo

83.   #ootdsubmit

84.   #outfit

85.   #outfitdiaries

86.   #outfitoftheday

87.   #outfitoftheday

88.   #outfitoftheday

89.   #photoshoot

90.   #revolveme

91.   #shoeoftheday

92.   #shoes

93.   #shoppinaddict

94.   #streetfashion

95.   #streetfashion

96.   #streetstyle

97.   #streetwear

98.   #style

99.   #styleblog

100.   #styleblogger

101.   #stylebook

102.   #stylecollective

103.   #styled

104.   #stylefiles

105.   #styleguide

106.   #styleinfluencer

107.   #styleinspo

108.   #styleiswhat

109.   #stylepost

The Best Hashtags for Luxury Lifestyle, Fitness&Sport, Fashion&Beauty on Instagram, Twitter, Facebook ....

110.   #stylish

111.   #teenagefashions

112.   #theeverygirl

113.   #todayimwearingthis

114.   #tomford

115.   #trend

116.   #trendy

117.   #vintage

118.   #whatimwearing

119.   #whatiwore

120.   #wiw

121.   #womensfashion

Catherine-chantal Marango

The Best Hashtags for Luxury Lifestyle, Fitness&Sport, Fashion&Beauty on Instagram, Twitter, Facebook ….

b.Fashion luxury brands hashtags

1. #Frederiqueconstant

2. #armani

3. #azzedinealaia

4. #balmain

5. #burberr

6. #callaluxury

7. #callaluxurylingerie

8. #calvinklein

9. #ChrisAireFineJewellery

10.   #courrège

11.   #Dolce&gabbana

Catherine-chantal Marango

12.   #frederiqueconstantboutique

13.   #gucci

14.   #hermès

15.   #Historic 1758

16.   #Hotdiamond

17.   #hotdiamondtrends

18.   #longchamp

19.   #MidaDJewellery

20.   #Mouawad

21.   #pacorabanne

22.   #pierrecardin

23.   #prada

Catherine-chantal Marango

24.   #tomford

25.   #thierrymugler

26.   #valentino

27.   #versace

28.   #vidalswim

29.   #wearableart

30.   #whitefieldartcollective

31.   #YUIMA NAKAZATO

c.fashionista hashtags

1. #hautecouture

Catherine-chantal Marango

2. #casualwear

3. #chaneltrendy

4. #classyfashion

5. #clothes

6. #clothesaddicted

7. #clothesaddiction

8. #clothesbrand

9. #currentlywearing

10.   #fashionable

11.   #fashionaddict

12.   #fashionblog

13.   #fashiondaily

14.   #fashiondiaries

15.   #fashiongram

16.   #fashionlover

17.   #fashionpost

18.   #fashionstyle

19.   #fblogger

20.   #garmentaddict

21.   #garments

22.   #instastyle

23.   #instyle

24.   #invogue

25.   #lookbook

Catherine-chantal Marango

26. #lookoftheday

27. #mylook

28. #ootdshare

29. #outfitoftheday

30. #outfitpost

31. #sportswear

32. #streetfashion

33. #streetwear

34. #styleblogger

35. #styleoftheday

36. #stylishchic

37. #tomford

Catherine-chantal Marango

The Best Hashtags for Luxury Lifestyle, Fitness&Sport, Fashion&Beauty on Instagram, Twitter, Facebook ....

38.   #topfashion

39.   #trendsetting

40.   #trendy

41.   #trendychic

42.   #trendyfashion

43.   #whatiwore

44.   #whatiworetoday

45.   #wiw

46.   #wiwt

d.Fashion show hashtags

1. #catwalk

Catherine-chantal Marango

The Best Hashtags for Luxury Lifestyle, Fitness&Sport, Fashion&Beauty on Instagram, Twitter, Facebook ….

2. #chanel

3. #dior

4. #fancycatwalk

5. #fancycatwalks

6. #fashiondaily

7. #fashiondesign

8. #fashiondesigner

9. #fashiongirl

10.   #fashionillustration

11.   #fashionistas

12.   #fashionlove

13.   #fashionlover

Catherine-chantal Marango

14.   #fashionlovers

15.   #fashionmodel

16.   #fashionoftheday

17.   #fashionphotography

18.   #fashionrunway

19.   #fashions

20.   #fashionshow

21.   #fashionstudy

22.   #fashionstyle

23.   #fashionstylist

24.   #fashionweek

25.   #ferragamo

The Best Hashtags for Luxury Lifestyle, Fitness&Sport, Fashion&Beauty on Instagram, Twitter, Facebook ….

26.   #gucci

27.   #hautecouture

28.   #highfashion

29.   #jeanpaulgauthier

30.   #lagerfeld

31.   #malemodel

32.   #malemodels

33.   #modelagency

34.   #modeling

35.   #modellife

36.   #modelling

37.   #models

Catherine-chantal Marango

38.   #runway

39.   #supermodels

40.   #valentino

41.   #versace

42.   #YSL

e)fashion blogger hashtags

1. #bblogger

2. # luxurylifestyleblogger

3. #beautyblogger

4. #bloggerlife

5. #bloggers

6. #bloggerstyle

7. #casualfashionblogger

8. #fashionable

9. #fashionblog

10. #fashionblogger

11. #fashiondiaries

12. #fashiongram

13. #fashioninspo

14. #fashioninspoblogger

15. #fashionkidswear

16. #fashionlook

17. #fashionmenswear

18. #fashionwomenswear

19.   #fblogger

20.   #inspo

21.   #instablog

22.   #instablogger

23.   #instastyle

24.   #lifestyleblogger

25.   #look

26.   #lookbook

27.   #lookoftheday

28.   #luxurylifestyle

29.   #menswear

30.   #outfitoftheday

31.   #shoes

32.   #streetfashion

33.   #streetwear

34.   #styleblogger

35.   #stylish

36.   #stylist

37.   #topfashionblogger

38.   #whatiwore

39.   #wiw

40.   #wiwt

e.Clothes, trends and styles hashtags

1. #academicdress

2. #activewear

3. #afrocentricfashion

4. #A-lineDress

5. #balldress

6. #Belgianfashion

7. #blazer

8. #blouse

9. #bohemiandress

The Best Hashtags for Luxury Lifestyle, Fitness&Sport, Fashion&Beauty on Instagram, Twitter, Facebook ….

10.   #clothes

11.   #cocktaildress

12.   #corset

13.   #costumejewellery

14.   #denim

15.   #empirestyle

16.   #Ethnicdress

17.   #ethnicestyle

18.   #eveningdress

19.   #extremefashion

20.   #fancydress

21.   #fashionable

Catherine-chantal Marango

22.   #fashionblog

23.   #fashiondiaries

24.   #fashiongram

25.   #fashioninspo

26.   #fashionpost

27.   #fashionstyle

28.   #futuristfashion

29.   #gloves

30.   #hautecouture

31.   #instastyle

32.   #instyle

33.   #invogue

34.   #jumperdress

35.   #littleblackdress

36.   #look

37.   #lookbook

38.   #lookoftheday

39.   #menstyle

40.   #menswear

41.   #militarystyle

42.   #outerwear

43.   #outfitoftheday

44.   #raincoat

45.   #ready-to-wear

46.   #retrostyle

47.   #shoes

48.   #streetfashion

49.   #streetwear

50.   #styleblogger

51.   #styleinspiration

52.   #stylish

53.   #trenchcoat

54.   #trend

55.   #trendalert

56.   #trending

57.   #trends

58.   #trendsetter

59.   #trendsetting

60.   #trendy

61.   #twinset

62.   #underwear

63.   #unisexclothing

64.   #vintagefashion

65.   #watches

66.   #wiw

67.   #wiwt

68.   #Working-Class Dress

Catherine-chantal Marango

The Best Hashtags for Luxury Lifestyle, Fitness&Sport, Fashion&Beauty on Instagram, Twitter, Facebook ….

f. Bags hashtags

1. #backpack

2. # fashionpurses

3. # Louis Vuitton Alma Bag

4. #bag

5. #bagaddict

6. #bagaholic

7. #baglady

8. #baglover

9. #bagoftheday

10.   #bags

Catherine-chantal Marango

The Best Hashtags for Luxury Lifestyle, Fitness&Sport, Fashion&Beauty on Instagram, Twitter, Facebook ….

11.   #bagshop

12.   #bagsoftpf

13.   #Balenciaga City Bag

14.   #birkinbag

15.   #botd

16.   #branded

17.   #Chanel Quilted Bag

18.   #chaneladdict

19.   #chanelclassic

20.   #chanellover

21.   #chanelquiltedbag

22.   #clutch

23.   #clutches

24.   #Croc-EffectLeatherbag

25.   #designerbags

26.   #Dior Saddle Bag

27.   #Diorbackpack

28.   #fashionbag

29.   #fashionbags

30.   #gucci

31.   #Gucci Quilted Shoulder Bag

32.   #guccibags

33.   #guccidionysushandlebag

34.   #guccihandlebag

35.   #ha

36.   #handbag

37.   #handbagcouture

38.   #handbags

39.   #handlebag

40.   #hermes

41.   #hermès

42.   #ladydiorbag

43.   #leather

44.   #leatherbag

45.   #longchamp

46.   #Longchamp Large Le PliageTote

47.   #longchampbags

48.   #louisvuitton

49.   #louisvuittonbags

50.   #luxurybag

51.   #luxuryleatherbags

52.   #LV Monogram Keepall Bag

53.   #pouch

54.   #pradadoubletote

55.   #purse

56.   #pursebop

57.   #sacdejour

58.   #sadlebag

59.   #saintlaurentsacdejour

60.   #shoulderbag

61.   #slingbag

62.   #The Chloé Faye Bag

63.   #Tote Bag

64.   #versace

65.   #wallet

66.   The Chanel Classic Flap

67.   The Louis Vuitton Neverfull

The Best Hashtags for Luxury Lifestyle, Fitness&Sport, Fashion&Beauty on Instagram, Twitter, Facebook ….

g.Jewellery hashtags

1. #accessories

2. #bling

3. #blingbling

4. #bracelet

5. #bracelets

6. #bulgari

7. #bulgarijewels

8. #cartier

9. #cartierjewels

The Best Hashtags for Luxury Lifestyle, Fitness&Sport, Fashion&Beauty on Instagram, Twitter, Facebook ….

10.   #chanel

11.   #chaneljewellery

12.   #charmbracelet

13.   #chopard

14.   #chopardjewellery

15.   #diamond

16.   #diamonds

17.   #earrings

18.   #finejewelry

19.   #gems

20.   #gemstone

21.   #gold

Catherine-chantal Marango

22.   #handmadejewelry

23.   #harrywintson

24.   #harrywintsonjewels

25.   #hiphopjewellery

26.   #hoophearings

27.   #initialnecklace

28.   #instajewelry

29.   #jewel

30.   #jeweller

31.   #jewellery

32.   #jewellerydesign

33.   #jewelry

34.   #jewelryaddict

35.   #jewelrydesigner

36.   #jewelrygram

37.   #jewels

38.   #letterrings

39.   #locket

40.   #magneticbracelet

41.   #multilayernecklace

42.   #necklace

43.   #pendant

44.   #pendantnecklace

45.   #ring

Catherine-chantal Marango

46.   #rings

47.   #silver

48.   #solarsystembracelet

49.   #swarovski

50.   #swarovskijewels

51.   #tiffany&co

52.   #tiffany&cojewels

h. Men's style hashtags

1. #menstagram

2. #dapper

3. #dappermen

The Best Hashtags for Luxury Lifestyle, Fitness&Sport, Fashion&Beauty on Instagram, Twitter, Facebook ….

4. #dapperstyleard

5. #gentleman

6. #gq

7. #guys

8. #handsome

9. #instaboy

10.   #instamen

11.   #malefashion

12.   #malemodel

13.   #masculinefashion

14.   #menfashion

15.   #meninlouisvuitton

Catherine-chantal Marango

The Best Hashtags for Luxury Lifestyle, Fitness&Sport, Fashion&Beauty
on Instagram, Twitter, Facebook ….

16.   #mensclothing

17.   #mensfashionpost

18.   #mensfashionreview

19.   #menslook

20.   #mensstyle

21.   #menstyle

22.   #menstyleguide

23.   #menswear

24.   #mensweardaily

25.   #menwithcasualstyle

26.   #menwithclass

27.   #menwithstreetstyle

Catherine-chantal Marango

28.   #menwithstyle

29.   #menwithstyle

30.   #stylish

31.   #suit

---

i. Shoes style hashtags

1. #OliverCabellLow 1

2. #adidas

3. #AdidasOriginals

4. #adidasshoes

5. #AdidasUltraBoost 20

6. #AdidasYeezyBoost

7. #BalenciagaBlackSpeed

8. #BalenciagaTrack 2

9. #BalmainB-Court

10.   #boots

11.   #casual

12.   #casual-chic

13.   #casualpumps

14.   #casualshoes

15.   #CelineTriompheGold

16.   #chanel

17.   #chanelballerinas

18.   #chanelblockheels

The Best Hashtags for Luxury Lifestyle, Fitness&Sport, Fashion&Beauty
on Instagram, Twitter, Facebook ….

19.   #chanelespadrilles

20.   #chic

21.   #classic

22.   #dolce&gabbanashoes

23.   #GoldenGooseSuperstar

24.   #GucciScreener

25.   #heels

26.   #higheels

27.   #highheels

28.   #igsneakercommunity

29.   #instakicks

30.   #instashoes

Catherine-chantal Marango

31.   #jordans

32.   #kicks

33.   #kicksonfire

34.   #kickstagram

35.   #KoioCapriCastagna

36.   #KoioGaviaBianco

37.   #KoioTempoBianco

38.   #LanvinBlack

39.   #longboots

40.   #LOUBOUTINCATACLOU.

41.   #louboutinshoes

42.   #MaisonMargielaFusion

43.   #nicekicks

44.   #nike

45.   #NikeAi Jordan

46.   #NikeAirForce 1 GTX

47.   #NikeAirMax270

48.   #NikeKillshot 2

49.   #nikeshoes

50.   #NikexSupreme

51.   #NikeZoomVaporfly

52.   #pantofel

53.   #pigallecourts

54.   #puma

55.   #pumashoes

56.   #pumps

57.   #SalomonXT-6

58.   #semiboots

59.   #shoes

60.   #shoestagram

61.   #sneaker

62.   #sneakerhead

63.   #sneakerheads

64.   #sneakernews

65.   #sneakers

66.   #solecollector

67.   #sporty

68.   #stylish

69.   #TomFordWarwick

70.   #valentino

71.   #Valentinoheels

72.   #VansLowTop

73.   #wedges

74.   #yeezy

75.   #YSLOpyum

#luxury presentation

Catherine-chantal Marango

The Best Hashtags for Luxury Lifestyle, Fitness&Sport, Fashion&Beauty
on Instagram, Twitter, Facebook ….

#luxury tableware

Catherine-chantal Marango

The Best Hashtags for Luxury Lifestyle, Fitness&Sport, Fashion&Beauty on Instagram, Twitter, Facebook ....

Catherine-chantal Marango

Chapter 5-The best beauty hashtags

a. Beauty general hashtags

1. #bblogger

2. #beautybasics

3. #beautyblogger

4. #blackbeauty

5. #casualbeauty

6. #caucasianbeauty

7. #chanelbeauty

8. #chicbeauty

9. #chinesebeauty

The Best Hashtags for Luxury Lifestyle, Fitness&Sport, Fashion&Beauty
on Instagram, Twitter, Facebook ….

10.   #classybeauty

11.   #cosmetics

12.   #diorbeauty

13.   #dressyourface

14.   #eyes

15.   #eyeshadow

16.   #frenchbeauty

17.   #glambeauty

18.   #gorgeous

19.   #hairstyle

20.   #hairstyles

21.   #hudabeauty

Catherine-chantal Marango

22.   #instabeauty

23.   #instamakeup

24.   #italianbeauty

25.   #jadorebeauty

26.   #lashes

27.   #lips

28.   #lipstick

29.   #makeupaddict

30.   #makeupforever

31.   #makeupjunkie

32.   #makeuplover

33.   #makeupyourface

The Best Hashtags for Luxury Lifestyle, Fitness&Sport, Fashion&Beauty on Instagram, Twitter, Facebook ….

34. #motd

35. #mua

36. #nailart

37. #natural

38. #naturalbeauty

39. #russianbeauty

40. #skincare

41. #styles

b. Beauty brands hashtags

c.

1. #anastasiabeverlyhills

Catherine-chantal Marango

The Best Hashtags for Luxury Lifestyle, Fitness&Sport, Fashion&Beauty on Instagram, Twitter, Facebook ....

2. #bareminerals

3. #beautyblender

4. #bobbibrown

5. #burberry

6. #chanel

7. #clarins

8. #clinique

9. #clinique

10. #covergirl

11. #covermx

12. #dermablend

13. #dermalogica

Catherine-chantal Marango

The Best Hashtags for Luxury Lifestyle, Fitness&Sport, Fashion&Beauty on Instagram, Twitter, Facebook ….

14.   #dior

15.   #elfcosmetics

16.   #elizabetharden

17.   #elizabetharden

18.   #esteelauder

19.   #gemey

20.   #givenchy

21.   #guerlain

22.   #hudabeauty

23.   #kiko

24.   #lancome

25.   #lauragellerbeauty

Catherine-chantal Marango

The Best Hashtags for Luxury Lifestyle, Fitness&Sport, Fashion&Beauty
on Instagram, Twitter, Facebook ....

26.   #lauramercier

27.   #loreal

28.   #mac

29.   #mac

30.   #maccosmetics

31.   #makeupforever

32.   #maybelline

33.   #nars

34.   #NYXelvon

35.   #nyxprofessionalmakeup

36.   #rimmel

37.   #sephora

Catherine-chantal Marango

38.   #shiseido

39.   #shueumera

40.   #sigmabeauty

41.   #smashbox

42.   #stila

43.   #tarte

44.   #urbandecay

45.   #versace

46.   #yvesrocher

47.   #yvessaintlaurent

Catherine-chantal Marango

c.Beauty bloggers hashtags

1. #anastasiabeverlyhills

2. #bblogger

3. #bbloggers

4. #beautyaddict

5. #beautyblog

6. #beautyblogger

7. #beautybloggerlife

8. #beautybloggers

9. #beautyguru

10.   #beautyjunkie

11.   #beautyproducts

12.   #cosmetics

13.   #hudabeauty

14.   #ilovemakeup

15.   #instabeauty

16.   #instablogger

17.   #instamakeup

18.   #lifestyleblogger

19.   #lipstick

20.   #maccosmetics

21.   #makeupaddict

22.   #makeupblogger

23.   #makeupjunkie

24.   #makeuplover

25.   #makeupmafia

26.   #makeupoftheday

27.   #motd

28.   #skincare

29.   #slave2beauty

30.   #wakeupandmakeup

d.Natural beauty hashtags

1. #cleanbeauty

2. #greenbeauty

3. #greenbeautybrands

The Best Hashtags for Luxury Lifestyle, Fitness&Sport, Fashion&Beauty on Instagram, Twitter, Facebook ….

4. #natural

5. #naturalbeauty

6. #naturalbeautybasic

7. #naturalbeautyblogger

8. #naturalbeautybrands

9. #naturalbeautycare

10. #naturalbeautychallenge

11. #naturalbeautyenhanced

12. #naturalbeautyisthebest

13. #naturalbeautylife

14. #naturalbeautylovers

15. #naturalbeautyoftheweek

16.   #naturalbeautyproduct

17.   #naturalbeautyproducts

18.   #naturalbeautyshoutouts

19.   #naturalbeautysupply

20.   #naturalbeautytips

21.   #naturalbeautyvibes

22.   #naturalbeautywithanaturalbooty

23.   #naturalhair

24.   #naturalhaircommunity

25.   #naturalhairdaily

26.   #naturalista

27.   #naturalskincare

28. #naturalskincare

29. #organicbeauty

30. #organicbeauty

31. #organicbeautybrands

32. #organicbeautybrands

33. #organicskincare

34. #skincare

35. #veganbeauty

36. #veganbeautybrands

e.Brows hashtags

1. #beautiful

2. #brows

3. #browsonfleek

4. #eyebrow

5. #eyebrowgame

6. #eyebrowgamestrong

7. #eyebrowgoals

8. #eyebrowmakeup

9. #eyebrown

10. #eyebrows

11. #eyebrowsdid

12. #eyebrowsdone

13. #eyebrowshaping

14. #eyebrowsonfleek

The Best Hashtags for Luxury Lifestyle, Fitness&Sport, Fashion&Beauty on Instagram, Twitter, Facebook ….

15.   #eyebrowsonpoint

16.   #eyebrowtattoos

17.   #eyebrowwigs

18.   #eyesmakeup

19.   #facelook

20.   #facemodel

21.   #fulleyebrows

22.   #hard-angled-archeyebrows

23.   #humanhaireyebrows

24.   #instabrows

25.   #instaeyebrows

26.   #instaface

Catherine-chantal Marango

27.   #instamakeup

28.   #longeyebrows

29.   #lookatthatface

30.   #mediumeyebrows

31.   #naturaleyebrows

32.   #newface

33.   #perfectbrows

34.   #perfecteyebrows

35.   #photooftheday

36.   #prettyface

37.   #prilaga

38.   #roundedeyebrows

39.   #shorteyebrows

40.   #softangledarcheyebrows

41.   #softeyebrows

42.   #s-shapedeyebrows

43.   #straighteyebrows

44.   #temporaryeyebrowstattoos

45.   #thickeyebrows

46.   #thineyebrows

47.   #thoseeyebrows

f.Face hashtags

1. #diamondface

2. #heart-shapedface

3. #longface

4. #ovalface

5. #pear-shapedface

6. #roundface

7. #squareface

g. eyes hashtags

1. #angeleyes

2. #almondshapeeyes

3. #blueeyes

4. #brighteyes

5. #browneyes

6. #closeseteyes

7. #darkeyes

8. #deepseteyes

9. #eye

10. #eyeball

11. #eyebrow

12. #eyebrows

13. #eyelashes

14. #eyes

15. #eyesmakeup

16. #greeneyes

17. #hoodedeyes

The Best Hashtags for Luxury Lifestyle, Fitness&Sport, Fashion&Beauty on Instagram, Twitter, Facebook ....

18.   #instaeyes

19.   #iris

20.   #monolid

21.   #myeye

22.   #prettyeyes

23.   #prilaga

24.   #pupil

25.   #roundeyes

26.   #vision

27.   #wideseteyes

h. eyelashes hashtags

1. #beautiful

Catherine-chantal Marango

The Best Hashtags for Luxury Lifestyle, Fitness&Sport, Fashion&Beauty on Instagram, Twitter, Facebook ....

2. #eyebrow

3. #eyelash

4. #eyelashes

5. #eyelashextensions

6. #eyesmakeup

7. #eyesshadow

8. #facelook

9. #facemodel

10.   #falseeyelashes

11.   #instaface

12.   #instamakeup

13.   #lash

Catherine-chantal Marango

14.   #lashaddict

15.   #lashart

16.   #lashartist

17.   #lashes

18.   #lashesfordays

19.   #lashextensions

20.   #lashlife

21.   #lashlove

22.   #lashmaker

23.   #lashpro

24.   #lashstylist

25.   #lashsuplies

Catherine-chantal Marango

26.   #lookatthatface

27.   #newface

28.   #prettyface

29.   #prilaga

30.   #visage

31.   #volumelashes

i. Hair hashtags

1. #balayage

2. #barber

3. #blonde

4. #braid

5. #brunette

6. #buns

7. #clips

8. #color

9. #curls

10.   #curly

11.   #curlyhair

12.   #eyes

13.   #finehair

14.   #haircolor

15.   #haircolour

16.   #haircut

17. #hairdo

18. #hairdresser

19. #hairextensions

20. #hairfashion

21. #hairofinstagram

22. #hairoftheday

23. #hairpiece

24. #hairstyle

25. #hairstyles

26. #hairstylist

27. #hairwraps

28. #humanhair

Catherine-chantal Marango

29.   #instahair

30.   #longhair

31.   #modernsalon

32.   #naturalhair

33.   #remyhumainhair

34.   #synthetichair

35.   #wavyhair

36.   #wigs

37.   Straighhair

j.Hairstyle hashtags

1. #bigcurls

2. #ballerinabun

The Best Hashtags for Luxury Lifestyle, Fitness&Sport, Fashion&Beauty on Instagram, Twitter, Facebook ….

3. #bob

4. #chichaircuts

5. #classyhaircuts

6. #coolhair

7. #curls

8. #curlsfordays

9. #curlsforthegirls

10.   #curlsonfleek

11.   #curlss

12.   #curly

13.   #curlygirls

14.   #curlygirlsrock

Catherine-chantal Marango

15. #curlyhair

16. #curlyhairdontcare

17. #curlyhairstyles

18. #curlyhead

19. #curlynatural

20. #cutlob

21. #cutshorthairstyles

22. #doublepony

23. #hair

24. #haircut

25. #hairdo

26. #hairfashion

27.   #hairideas

28.   #hairofinstagram

29.   #hairoftheday

30.   #hairstyle

31.   #hairstyles

32.   #headband

33.   #instafashion

34.   #layeredhaircuts

35.   #loosecurls

36.   #medium-length-hairstyles

37.   #naturalcurls

38.   #perfectcurls

39. #pixicut

40. #ponytail

41. #prilaga

42. #style

k. makeup hashtags

1. #base

2. #bblogger

3. #beautyblogger

4. #concealer

5. #contour

6. #cosmetic

7. #eyebrows

8. #eyeliner

9. #eyes

10. #eyeshadow

11. #foundation

12. #glitter

13. #gloss

14. #highlight

15. #instabeauty

16. #instamakeup

17. #lash

18. #lashes

19.   #lips

20.   #lipstick

21.   #makeupaddict

22.   #makeupforever

23.   #makeupjunkie

24.   #makeuplover

25.   #mascara

26.   #motd

27.   #palettes

28.   #powder

29.   #primers

30.   #wakeupandmakeup

Catherine-chantal Marango

The Best Hashtags for Luxury Lifestyle, Fitness&Sport, Fashion&Beauty on Instagram, Twitter, Facebook ….

1. **Nails hashtags**

1. #gel

2. #bluenails

3. #colornails

4. #designsnails

5. #fallnails

6. #gelnails

7. #gelpolish

8. #glitternails

9. #graynails

10. #instanails

Catherine-chantal Marango

11.   #manicure

12.   #mattenails

13.   #moodnails

14.   #nail

15.   #nailaddict

16.   #nailart

17.   #nailartaddict

18.   #nailartist

19.   #nailcare

20.   #naildesign

21.   #nailenhancements

22.   #nailpolish

Catherine-chantal Marango

The Best Hashtags for Luxury Lifestyle, Fitness&Sport, Fashion&Beauty on Instagram, Twitter, Facebook ….

23.   #nailpromote

24.   #nails2inspire

25.   #nailsart

26.   #nailsdone

27.   #nailslove

28.   #nailsofinstagram

29.   #nailsoftheday

30.   #nailsoftheweek

31.   #nailsonpoint

32.   #nailspolish

33.   #nailstagram

34.   #nailswag

Catherine-chantal Marango

35.   #naturalnails

36.   #notd

37.   #opi

38.   #pinknails

39.   #polish

40.   #purplenails

41.   #rosegoldnails

42.   #shellac

43.   #sparklenails

44.   #sportnails

45.   #summernails

46.   #twotoonenails

47.   #unhas

48.   #whitenails

49.   #winternails

50.   Acrylicnails

m. skincare hashtags

1. #antiaging

1. #<u>BeautyAwardWinners</u>

2. #beautycare

3. #cellumination

4. #clearskin

5. #collagen

The Best Hashtags for Luxury Lifestyle, Fitness&Sport, Fashion&Beauty on Instagram, Twitter, Facebook ....

6. #cosmetics

7. #esthetician

8. #eyecream

9. #face

10.   #facial

2. #Facialmasks

3. #facialmists

4. #Facialmoisturisers

5. #Facialoils

6. #facialpolishes

7. #facialscrubs

8. #Facialserums

Catherine-chantal Marango

11. #facialskincare

9. #facialtoners

12. #glow

13. #glowingskin

14. #healthyskin

15. #intaskincare

16. #mask

10. #<u>Mensskincare</u>

17. #naturalskincare

18. #organicfacialskincare

19. #organicskincare

20. #organicskincareproducts

Catherine-chantal Marango

21. #selfcareday

22. #serum

23. #skin

24. #skincare

25. #skincareaddict

26. #skincareaman

27. #skincarejunkie

11. #Skincarekits

28. #skincarelover

29. #skincareproducts

30. #skincareroutine

31. #skincaretips

32. #skinfood

33. #skinrejuvenation

34. #skintreatment

12. #Stressedskinsaviours

m. Plastic surgery and Aesthetic Surgery hashtags

1. #injectablefillers

2. #acculift

The Best Hashtags for Luxury Lifestyle, Fitness&Sport, Fashion&Beauty on Instagram, Twitter, Facebook ….

3. #acnetreatment

4. #Antiagingtreatments

5. #beardtransplantation

6. #beardtransplantationtreatment

7. #bodylaesthetics

8. #Botilinumtoxininjection

9. #breastaesthetics

10.   #breastreduction

11.   #breastsimplants

12.   #breatsurgery

13.   #buttimplants

14.   #cheekimplants

Catherine-chantal Marango

15. #chinimplants

16. #cosmeticsurgery

17. #demalfillers

18. #eyebagsurgery

19. #eyebrowtransplantation

20. #eyebrowtransplantationtreatment

21. #eyecontouraesthetics

22. #facelifting

23. #facialaesthetics

24. #facialcontouringsurgery

25. #facialplasticsurgery

26. #facialreconstruction

27.   #fatgrafting

28.   #fillerstreatment

29.   #foreheadlift

30.   #hairtransplant

31.   #hairtransplantation

32.   #hairtransplantationtreatment

33.   #implant

34.   #jawimplants

35.   #juvederm

36.   #lipaugmentationtreatment

37.   #liposuction

38.   #lipsaesthetics

39.   #medicalaesthetics

40.   #nosejob

41.   #oxypeelix

42.   #radiesse

43.   #restylane

44.   #Rhinoplasty

45.   #skinrejuvenation

46.   #skinspottreatment

47.   #threadlifting

48.   #tummytuck

The Best Hashtags for Luxury Lifestyle, Fitness&Sport, Fashion&Beauty on Instagram, Twitter, Facebook ....

Catherine-chantal Marango

The Best Hashtags for Luxury Lifestyle, Fitness&Sport, Fashion&Beauty
on Instagram, Twitter, Facebook ....

Catherine-chantal Marango

The Best Hashtags for Luxury Lifestyle, Fitness&Sport, Fashion&Beauty on Instagram, Twitter, Facebook ....

Catherine-chantal Marango

Conclusion

I hope the first volume of the encyclopedia of the best universal hashtags helps you extend your reach on Instagram, Twitter, Facebook, Tik Tok, get more engagement and popularity on your posts, get rid of the hashtag fatigue and find the best engagement opportunities. For a full reach and engagement, do consider the reading of the three other volumes of the encyclopedia.

If you have any question, suggestion or feedback, please contact me: info@personalfrenchteacher.com

Catherine-chantal Marango

The Best Hashtags for Luxury Lifestyle, Fitness&Sport, Fashion&Beauty
on Instagram, Twitter, Facebook ....

Catherine-chantal Marango

The Best Hashtags for Luxury Lifestyle, Fitness&Sport, Fashion&Beauty
on Instagram, Twitter, Facebook ….

Catherine-chantal Marango

The Best Hashtags for Luxury Lifestyle, Fitness&Sport, Fashion&Beauty on Instagram, Twitter, Facebook ....

Catherine-chantal Marango

About the Author

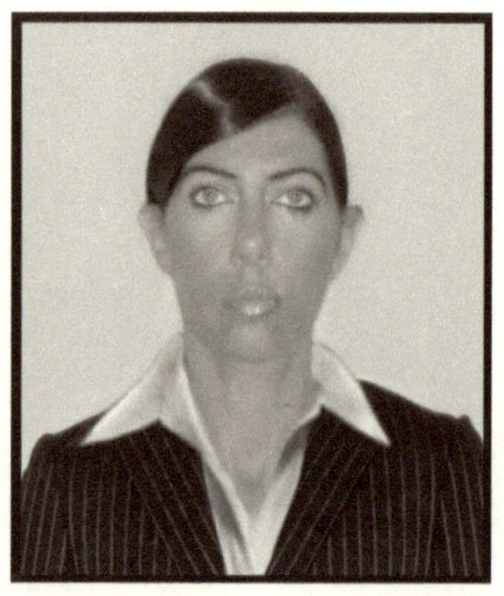

Catherine- Chantal Marango is a highly trained French multilingual professional who has many years of experience as a successful Foreign Language Expert and pedagogical pyschologist, working in Nice, France.

Catherine-chantal Marango

She celebrates with her Mediterranean enthusiasm 10 years being in the Language business.

Successfully running her linguistic company Personal French Teacher (www.personalfrenchteacher.com), she has worked with thousands of high-qualified global students seeking a real language improvement from general to specific purposes.

Her real-world experience, multilingualism, extensive education , pragmatic connection and pedagogical psychology makes her the excellent choice to help you speak the world with flying colors.

Now, by reading her books and taking her courses, it is your chance to be a real success!!!

Catherine-chantal Marango